Before the Heart Went Down

Selected Poems by Robert Billings

(with 12 previously uncollected works)

Selected by Sharon Berg

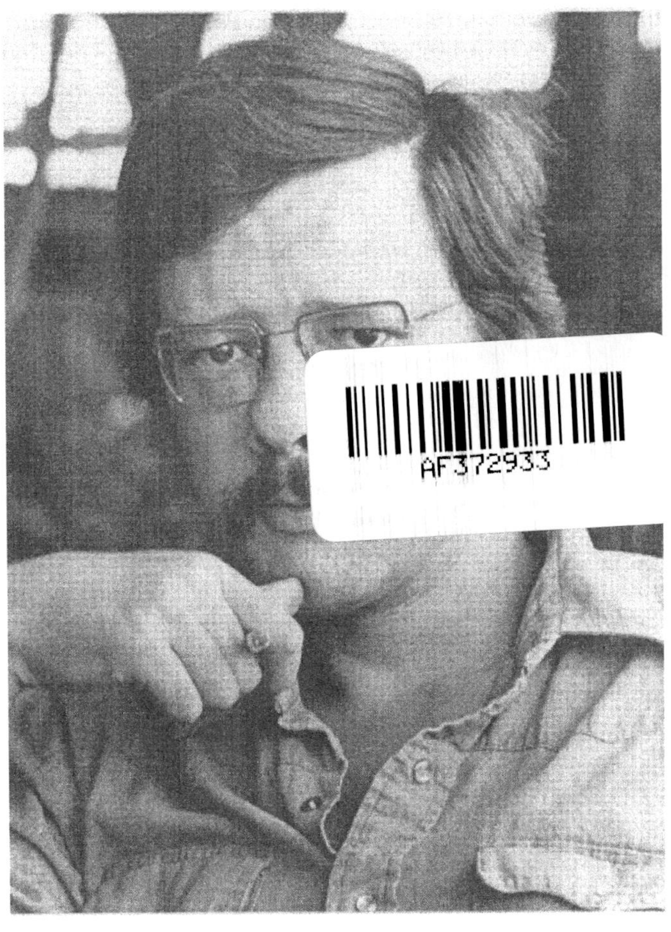

**Before the Heart Went Down
Selected Poems by Robert Billings**
Selected by Sharon Berg
© Robert Billings (poems)

ISBN # 978-93-90202-57-7

Published by Cyberwit.net
HIG 45, KAUSHAMBI KUNJ, KALINDIPURAM,
ALLAHABAD - 211011 (U.P.) INDIA +(91) 9415091004
www.cyberwit.net/

In remembrance of Robert Billings
& for all authors whose unpublished works
are unprotected & lost when they pass over.
There are too many.

4

Contents

Trying to Dream for My Son (1984)

Northern Poems: Where the Heart Catches Its Breath (1986)

The Revels (1986)

The White City Poems (1985-86)

8

Prologue: A Self-Portrait in Words

This book presents a self-portrait of Robert, different than most readers will hold of him before its release. That's the power of collecting an author's best pieces into a single book. It's also the power of reflecting on all that Robert Billings made happen for Canadian writing during his lifetime. His writing speaks for him.

How did this book come to be? It started with a sheaf of ten poems that Robert gave to me while we were dating (1985-1986). They are poems that I was determined to do the right thing with. In this book, you are presented with the best of Robert Billings, the poet, the man, and his heart.

Sharon Berg

Robert Billings sitting with Brynna Kirsten Rene Berg, Winter 1985

A Brief Biography of Robert Billings

Robert Kilborn Billings was born in Niagara Falls, Ontario in 1949. He disappeared around Halloween and passed an unknown length of time before his body was found in the Niagara River in the Spring of 1987. His high school friend, Michael Clarkson, confirms that while he was always amiable, he never felt entirely comfortable in the social world and experienced a lonely existence during his school years. He collected a Masters degree in English from the University of Windsor, where he was the Assistant Editor for *Poetry Windsor* magazine (1977-1978). It was during this time he released his first book, **blue negatives** (1977, Fiddlehead Poetry Books). He then became a Ph.D. candidate in Canadian Literature at Queen's University, where he was also Assistant Editor of *Quarry* (1977-1979). When **The Elizabeth Trinities** (1980, Penumbra Press) was released, Robert was working as a freelance editor, but he also held the position of Reviews Editor for *Waves*.

Robert married Anne Vaughan Evans and they had a son named Tom. When **A Heart Of Names** (1983, Mosaic Press) was published, they lived in Toronto. Robert was a stay-at-home father and continued to work as a literary editor. He was deeply troubled by personal demons, as is revealed in **Trying To Dream For My Son** (1984, Aureole Point Press). Yet, in his public life, he'd gained respect from the literary establishment as the Editor of *Poetry Canada Review* and *Poetry Toronto*. He was also elected as Vice-President of *The League of Canadian Poets* and some say, if he had lived, he would have been the next President.

However, he struggled with issues in his private life which resulted partly from a separation from his wife in early 1985. In the summer of 1985, he spent six weeks in Sault Ste. Marie, where he created an over-sized pamphlet called **Northern Poems: Where The Heart Catches Its Breath**

(1986 Penumbra Press/Northward Journal). By this time, he'd long established himself as a literary critic, authoring several pieces that focused on the new generation of Canadian poets. The final book published by Robert is **The Revels** (1986, Porcupine's Quill).

Robert began to work on **The White City Poems** (1985-86) on or around Christmas Day in 1985. Few of those poems survive from a much larger manuscript that he worked on. Later, he began a series of poems about torture for PEN Canada and Amnesty International, meeting with Bruce Meyer for lunch just two or three weeks before he disappeared, and talking about those poems with great excitement. However, as happens in the lives of too many authors, one's last manuscripts are not always protected from a bad end. After he passed, most of his unpublished work was simply tossed out.

Robert died by suicide at Niagara Falls, Ontario, Canada, sometime after Halloween 1986. The exact date is unknown. His body was discovered in the river below Niagara Falls in the Spring of 1987.

His wonderful poetry, collected here, speaks of his life, his deep connection to nature, his insights as he searched for love, his bruised heart, and the struggle he had with his demons.

1

blue negatives
(1977)

Invocation

There is a darkness
I try to tell you about —

It is between us,
Between us and our lovers,
Between us and our children,
Even between us and the embrace

The spirits are close,
But cautious
From long experience:

They hide their faces
And go dumb
Each time a touch of being
On being is not admitted.

We say we want them back.

Jill

Your pale
exotic
    whiteness
like some moonbeams
    in soft black rooms
confuses me

falling down
the stairs
on my way out
I felt you laugh
and hold me close
one more second

Clare Dancing

When they hear your name
People see you on tea-chairs,
Skirt folded over glued knees...

But the poems about you
They were written with the Stones
You dancing by yourself in the front room
Of that house on Somerset
The one they tore down in the spring

The manuscripts have titles at the top
"Shelter", "Bleed", "Silver", "Live with Me"

The house would have fallen down by itself
The green bank clock on the corner
Was right four times we looked at it
And it snowed the day I wrote
About the blood on my face.

You are dancing now -
Will I brush your cheek like the first time?

Leaves for Karen

Not to him who seeks it with fervor,
Nor to him who seeks it without hope,
Will the multifarious vision come:

Its refracting-glass is the moon's orbit,
That shatters the magnificence of the matrix
Into zodiac and spectrum;

And whatever the character of zenith,
The nadir directly under where we stand
Is but a nascent glimmer of the gloss.

So you who seek a still truth and calm,
Take a lesson from the leaves:
All summer they watch the wind
And conceive the plans of slaves;
Only to become in Autumn ruffianly bands
Musing on glory and a daring leader.

Kingston

Ann On Our Last Night In Frankfurt

Is it because this woman cannot stomach
Degas' *Two Dancers On The Stage*
That she can grasp her ponytail in her left hand
And throw it over her back so provocatively?

It is not well-made: the locks fall carelessly
As if the mane were moulded by wind,
Mirror and comb set aside
In homage to Venetian courtesans.

Or is it because her lovers come to believe
Themselves initiates of Dionysus
When they realize her loosened hair gushes
Like blood from a bull's throat?

But tonight she seems incapable of mere ritual.
As she moves among these white walls
And casts out the sigh that regains her freedom,
It is impossible to tell
If she walks on floor or alter
And if the Main is barrier or carpet.

She is barely dressed in blue,
And so resembles a savior
I am afraid to look at her hands.

Jenny In A Small Garden, Augsburg

Sky, blue and high, small
Trees and pool, accustomed
To the fountain's spray, goldfish;

Bells of the cathedral sound
Colours, drown Luther's sermon,
Sinning bravely;

An excited man with steady
Eyes, old Hylas, gesturing —

Worried Herkules, nearby,
Stands among the traffic
Of Maximilianstrasse …

Arrested in this moment,
Marmorean, she stands small,
Fading colours longing
For less light, her
Perfect composure mossy
As the Roman ruins.

Autumn In Vienna

In Vienna, Autumn is four weeks
Of Sunday afternoons. The rain
From the Alps stays away,
And hints of Beethoven and Mozart
Scurry between old buildings like
A king's as-yet-unofficial mistress

The streets are full of golden and red
Whirlwinds which, except for the silence,
Could be soldiers, clean-shaven,
Gaudy and proud, congratulating each other.

A carriage goes by: women
With parasols and bobbed hair,
Or grotesque white wigs
Who pretend they don't know
The touch and taste of flesh.

If you walk in the Strauss Park,
There is a lady in a long,
Pale-blue dress who seems
To waltz with a captain
Across the cobblestones
Of Dr. Karl Lueger Reise
To sip tea and cinnamon
From tiny, crafted cups.

And just when you're sure
They're real and now,
Julie may slip her hand
From yours to point at
the Hofburg balcony from which
Hitler claimed this city.

On Karen Reading Yeats This Afternoon

It is Wednesday, December,
a cold midweek bleached blue
with sky and psalm-gold light
that moves carefully (if you watch it)
across the small side-room.

The curtain, striped brown with red,
is pulled back on the right
and the light bursts through, white,
fresh with might and new snow.

In a corner you sit crouched up in a chair;
fingers, clean and perfect with water,
pressing my Yeats against your knees,
reading *The Rose*.

Your yellow robe is just tight enough —
as light moves across to you
I can see the verity shadows hide,
and know the stillness sun has brought you unbidden.

When people, outside, move by laughing, bursting,
with gay conversation of what and then,
I see your brows crinkle,
wrinkles of your forehead
as you turn slightly, uncomfortable
in a frown of sidewalks and recess.

So I take this room away for you:
to a mountain in Austria,
colder and crueler with peace;
to Vancouver over-looking
the Channel, white-capped and strong;
to Ireland, in the country,

faeries and old men
slow with stubble and pipe …
But it does not do;
it just does not do.

In the stillness of this sun, of this light,
mingling you with snow and sky,
you are yellow, shimmering,
and O, so blue with quiet
as your fingers turn a page
and your eyes are nowhere at all.

2

The Elizabeth Trinities
(1980)

The Legend of the Pike

A lake in Northern Ontario

I

Even this comes from stillness.
Before the boats, fire and the spear,
in a world of intelligible speech,
it has seen rock, sky and pine forest,
blood shed by blood into water —
that gush of gut over its snout —
and its own blood flapped out
onto rock and bear's jowls.
All this and more with fish-eye:
Curious, open, fearing. Swipe
and clamp of jaws held life
struggling, seized, impotent,
against that awe and dread —
as if in those clamped worlds
some necessity lay, was known too well
or seen once, beforehand, and haunted.

This has always been
dead serious about life:
from the first womb's gush of water,
it became easy to recognize the enemy,
its born-with smile a leer
in the name of water and camaraderie
here against what is. First,
family, then plant, perch,
all other life was the curse
to be cursed with jaws & gulp
that brought blood to blood.

But stillness. Even now it leaps

to evening. All day spent
in a brood and languor,
recessed, in tensed wildness
from the insistence of light,
suddenly flipped outside the world
into glare or sharp shadow:
the killing air is a joy, a threat
to be toyed with as a trout
that has whipped itself a last time
from its insensate grasp, floats there,
half-over, vincible.

Such was the pride of this birth:
to know at once oneness, invincible,
to leap before the ice
into August sunsets
and against life,
articulate in that joy
only the meaning
of the water's dark & the pine.

And the lake, still, is cold:
from the pike-heart cold blood
seeped, spread in the waves' wash
over minnow, into the badger's mouth
and the clawed deer; hawk-heart
and jays gashed the air,
as they do now,
in glare and shadow,
their scorn and eye's smirk
jealous against squirrel
and intruder — coldness
dogged up and down the beach,
a portent against any stillness.

But only the pike is pure
in this death. Only it,

alone, immote, waits
adrift in stupor and brotherhood
for bass or trout or sunfish
to bring it glistening;
its machine-head and heart
against life is all the others'
wonder, and melody; its
swish close by and its
leaps from the world
are born in its deeper instinct,
its first wildness;
and what possibility
its jaws can not clamp
never had life.

And its world is complete: a pike's head wrapped in news
paper rots in the August sun: the tricked god.

II

But it was not always so.

Climbing the cliff
that leaps from Lost Bay's side,
we pause to get breath back,
and look down
on what once was pure.

The water just deep enough
to canoe, and still,
the lake's currents
and waves chop suddenly,
in a moment, left
and as if they had never been.
The horseshoe shoreline
trapped sound:

whippoorwill song & crows' caw
echoed from the cliff;
& turtle splashes,
Profound, or frenzied
Against our canoe's impudence.
The prow glided water-lilies
away, minnows & small perch
did sudden half-turns,
their water-eyes
just spawned,
saw more fear than
those brains could grasp.
Now, half-up
through the birch and maple cliff,
we remember the pike that did not move
from the prow, but held,
defiant, or sure of us,
in a welter of minnows,
its fish-eye & gulp
thankless for the fear
that made them
forget it and easy prey.

We understand its boredom, would,
on an old day, have made sacrifice
there where we paused for breath:
the stench & smoke
of rescued flesh would waft down
on the bay's circling winds
over the god's world —
and it would be pleased;
and us no longer afraid
it would rise again
and, with that fish-eye
now ablaze & sharp
as a dried pine-needle,
come for us & our families,

seek from our birch-witch
pleasure, life, rot that wood
with gills' gulp & slime
so arrows would curve off
before our enemies' heart.
And as the badger flesh burned
with the badger's growl,
our water-shaggy, gnarled fish
would dance & chant
with his smeared body
and from his deep heart
the god's song, of how,
after the beginning,
it called about it
its family to be
adored and lay law; how
it quivered in shallow water
between two sunfish,
and gaped awe & dread
before that wide-eyed life:
bear and otter, jay and beaver
and crow were all
struck stone before that stare.

The regal salmon, permitted,
invoked speech; the god
twisted its smirk, its
gorge gulped, rose, invoked
womb, water and jaws.

A muskrat and a hawk,
the one's claws rammed
down the other's throat,
were dragged between two weasels
to the water's edge, lit
upon, scourged with teeth
to growls and caws

and song, until
they were finally still
before the god's eyes,
and a gulp rose, proclaiming,
'I call womb, water & jaws
which you shall not betray.

'It is for this
I have allowed you to be.

'Learn: this muskrat
is the hawk's' it
was surprised by the shadow,
turned so my claws missed.

'It should not.
You will not.

'And this hawk,
ignoble air-life,
was too stunned
by the sun to see.

'Learn: a sure aim,
Unblended, dark, mine
Against life.

'You shall know my eyes.
You shall know simplicity
in my layered jaws.'

Perch tried to hide
their brightness; bears
longed for grace,
snakes for fins;
lackey bass gulped
prayers to be perfect.

'I banish this muskrat
to shallow water: may
foxes find it soon.'

'And this hawk
I give to the crows:
may their darkness last.'

The god ceased.

A chorus of owls
hooted heart's blood:
heart's fear, as if vanquished,
bowed off, the two sunfish
moving against it —
fear of those two traitors
was pure.

              And the pike held,
gulping for the bass
the salmon led close.

But we do not make sacrifice.
We blow smoke-rings
and watch the butts spiral
down to still world.

We would not hear again
how the last council
would not be renewed,
& how our smeared fish
would grovel on pine needles
and urge us back to water.

We would not remember
this place: how

the spear's thrust felt
in the old man's chest;
or how, that first time,
the pike's breath caught
as it flayed on the shaft.

But we see it
leap far below us,
there is something
in its awkward arch
and glistening
we will remember
as we remember
our families
and the loons' cries
at evening.

An hour away from that clamped world, we hang our
clothes on a birch-branch and jump joy, dive,
hold breath, make love under a pine.

3

A Heart Of Names
(1983)

Cayuga

---

for Roger, Kilborn, Catherine

i

1924
my father did cannonballs
slapping explosions of water
into the Grand River twenty
winding miles upstream
from Lake Erie —

the fat kid in a Rockwell illustration

Once jumped deliberately
onto Bill Colter
felt the give of shoulders
and neck under his clenched knees

was dunked pushed under
by Bill's famous
perfectly tanned legs

1982
the old Colter house is For Sale again
woodworm in the porch
$1200 to heat last winter

And the river is green mud
mosquitos, two punks smoking
up on the old diving board

Every Christmas there was a card
from Bill, a two-page
letter with fondest love

1980
my father read it from arm's length:
within the hour told me again
he could see Bill's legs
like they were coming out of the sun

ii

Bulrushes under the railway bridge

I'm 14
mad at church
mad at the 60-mile drive here
every other Sunday
mad at everything

I'm down at the river
to escape tea and
chatter in the den
snoring in the parlour
I know *The Hamilton Spectator*
is crumpled across my father's chest

dragonflies buzz me
I snap off a bulrush
and swat wildly

Then
more cunning
crouch in the high grass
and make one quick arc
with all my might

break blue wings in the mud

I climb the long hill back to the house
back to another chicken supper
more hot apple pie & mild cheddar
Silverwood's French Vanilla

Again this week my grandfather
is chewing so loudly I move
my chair as far as I can to the left

On the way home I'm thinking
how jagged I made those wings

stare into oncoming headlights
the whole 60 miles

iii

The day my grandmother voted Tory
she wore a yellow dress
with huge white flowers
a brimless straw hat
and carried a parasol

Three weeks earlier
in the gazebo beside the lawn-tennis court
she poured tea for Liberal Jim Allan
and fourteen ladies from the church

My father remembered crumbs of apple cake
in the grass
under the cushions of chairs

Grit born bred and married
she kept the secret seventeen years
went silent left the room
whenever politics was raised

1972
she came to believe all light meant fire
fell the steps to the larder reaching
for a switch she couldn't see

To her deathbed
even now
in fun branded the traitor

I am still learning how to remember her:
defiant, mad, broken

I am still learning how to admit
the afternoon of my grandfather's laugh
and averted eyes
iv

My father born a week into the war

In the courthouse
farmboys who would have been men
he knew
knew the sons & daughters of
enlisting

I have read their names ranks
on a statue between stuffed canons

My grandmother remembered nothing
but heat in the middle bedroom
motionless white curtains
& a painting of the homestead 1848
on the wall she arched her neck back to

My grandfather's memories were faces
shaken hands slapped backs

1969
I have a beard
& dirty hair to my shoulders

He tells me he led his choir
lustily
in "Onward Christian Soldiers"

then sipped tea as usual
in the Church Hall
between 12:15 & 1
He crosses his legs
lights another cigarette
tells me he cannot remember how
many years his soul has been lukewarm

v

The master bedroom
has been filled with half-light
as long as I can remember

I was always afraid of the closet
the stuck doorknob
the dark creak of hinges

Once I watched my father open it
from under his elbow saw
outlines of boxes
shadow so dark
I could see no walls

After the second funeral
I open it myself and find
Lay of the Last Minstrel
(Copp Clark, 1902)

palm-sized copies of *Evangeline*
and *Silas Marner*

at the bottom of a box
white cameos of Victoria R
Edward and two Georges

I overturn a cardboard wardrobe
The smell of mothballs tumbles
out with purple dresses
baggy trousers
eight pairs of spats

I bump my head on a shelf
wince at a sliver in my knee

For days I have a stiff back from bending

vi

My first nightmare
was Mrs Colter's fox fur
its head still on
glass eyes, a hard black snout
draped over the spinning wheel my
great grandmother had sat behind
in the best-lit corner of the homestead

1957
I'm 8   I poke 2 fingers
in the eyes, put a hand
can't get my head into its mouth
I stroke its back, make
its claws scratch a cousin's face

I remember blood and iodine
my cousin screaming in the kitchen
Twenty years later
over tea at the same kitchen table
I look for the scar as she
talks quietly of executions
of being able to hear shots
thousands of miles away

I tell her I dreamed of a fox
with a mouth as big as a city

She tells me my own story
says it's right here

vii

1971
my grandmother remembered this

The Kohler brothers
circling and whistling their cattle
onto the *Queen City Queen*

By sundown
drunk in the Campbell House

That evening she joined the promenade
of white clothes and straw hats
along the east bank
watched half-naked Negroes
glowing as they pitched
shovel after shovel of coal
into the red furnace

Buffalo was two days away
two days of stoking
and scraping cowshit
over the side

At dawn
Pa Kohler's wagon
rattling over the wooden bridge
woke everyone

1911
from the window of that
half-lit room
she saw his sons
stretched flat
tied down
in the back of the wagon

For 60 years she said their horses
walking behind
were palomino angels in the sunrise

viii

30 feet from cracked asphalt
potholes
behind the windbreak
for Arvin Johnson's farm
one grey marble headstone
with two names

It is a minute's drive
from the church where I was
christened, my aunt
married to her captain

1943
It is the place I learned not to
believe, the place I carried my
first casket out of
There is ivy to the roof
on every wall
and still
women in purple dresses with
tiny white flowers
drink tea every Sunday at
12:15

I am alive
I am naming my weapons
I am learning how to curve around
edges, how to ride the circumference of
seasons with a slack or
steady grip

And I believe in this —

how I have stood here twice before
with my hands folded in front of me,
both times watched sun and long shadows
spread over the headstones
and they are here today
as I reach down quickly
and pick up my son two
baby steps onto the grave

Migration

I will see this again   The sun beginning
to pull earth's green up into birches

I had come to believe the world
is the window that deceives the bird:
cracked glass; hysteria in a shadow

Is this the year I will fall in love
with chicory beside a gravel road,
a river?

And memory: it is wind through feathers
Or is it wings that are taking the heart
into a flame blown whiter and whiter?

Warm air   Smell of ice melting
The heart accepts one small crack at a time

The Paul Kane House: Wellesley Street E.

I walk close to the walls
carefully run my fingers along
the yellow brick he chose

But I cannot reach him

two girls smoke in the alley
music, shouts from a balcony
of the high rise in his back yard

1852 he named this
Miss-qua-Kany Lodge
a closed space to sit
in southern light through tall windows
and remembers a sky so huge
he sometimes made it invisible

to map a precise geometry
for "Winter-traveling in Dogsled"

or the exact shape of a beast
blinded by running and fear

Sometimes there were the colours
of villages built in dust:
the dogs and fresh carcasses
women mixing paint in clay bowls
or maybe, suddenly from a dark corner
the straight mouth and narrow eyes
of Tom-Ma-Kus looking through him again

These and more he gave final shape
between daily visits to the Island

requests to do a fierce portrait
(head-dress, blood in the eyes)
for the bric-a-brac wall
of a gentleman's house by the lake

Now, boarded up
surrounded by renovation, low rise
office space, fast food
it stands back from this street
of traffic and shouldering crowds

the sidewalk where every night
women pass on their way
to narrow beds or parked cars

The lawn is dirty and dead grass
garbage strewn by alley-dogs

I step gingerly on the back porch:

my foot goes through easily
as an arrowhead into flesh

or as wind at 59 below
cracks a man's skin open
through buckskin and the shaggiest robe

Flowers at My Father's Funeral

They are pulled from the hearse
and dropped in a line along
the east wall of the canopy

It is minus 23 Celsius
and wind from the north-west

Half-way through
the bald minister's monotone
just after his
stumble over the name
a gust of wind scatters
petals of a yellow rose
out over the snow —

cheerleaders
I think
cheerleaders doing cartwheels
in the name of that dead god
or else ecstatic fairies stealing
the soul under our eyes

I cannot bring my stare back
to that brown coffin   My hands
want to be wings and join
that graceful dodge of headstones
that bright dance to the woods

And later from the warm limousine
The last memory where nothing moves —

flowers and pots and bright paper
piled on another grave:
a lump of frozen rainbow

Anne With a Guitar Singing

Only on bright days
on streets I walk down slowly
or at evening in the quiet house
in the first seconds of rain
I climb mountains
I was carried up as a child

It is sometimes your voice
the held pitch of a note
I did not expect to hear
in this life
sometimes the silence between two notes
or the words
you put side by side
like the woman who invented
darkness to match what she saw

I think it is the silence
I am descended from
I live now in attempts
at not moving a muscle
until I have heard everything
you will or will not tell me
before the rain stops
the next cloud rolls in
like a dog barking
a door slamming
as you play

Epiphanies of the First Cold Day

1

I thought there was nothing in the fields of light
that was not there in darkness

After breakfast in a quiet house
surrounded by pastures of new frost
my heart crouches believing
the next sound will be
something it can sing

2

This is my persistent nightmare

I jump into a shallow river
My feet sink in mud to
mid-calf, the top of
my head just
breaks the surface

It's November
Too soon for ice
to preserve me

At noon I warm my hands at the apples
Ripening on the window sill

3

The smell of cold through an open window

On the corner of my desk
is a print of the mother-goddess
in a black plastic frame

Syria
Third century BC
The guidebook defines
Civilization
Means living together

Sometimes a glancing blow
is the back of my wife's hand
slowly down my thigh

4

And so it comes back to this

In Munich 1974
a man in a bar
said a cormorant
dropping from a cliff
is the soul of
whatever flung this
earth on the sea

Midnight on the highway through Perth County
wearing sunglasses against the headlights
I bite through the skin of an apple

Greenwood Hill in Winter: 1848

Snow Full moon
Windows painted with warm light

This is my frozen history:
a heart of names behind stone walls
a snake-fence rilled with snow

And a man — cousin, grandfather? —
who hunches from the barn to the house
His cloud of breath comes down to me

I have stood up in the world
with my arms awry, with a shortness of words
I have the heritage of a blind man

And you, among trees bent by a hundred years
of wind down the valley — are you one of the men
who wanted to hold everything in one hand?

I want one distance to come to me across a field
I want it to be singing

Some days there are more snowflakes than words
I will speak all my life Smell of cold air
is a thing I will miss most from the earth

Blizzard in April

A senseless end of thaw
Wind from all directions

at once (how
the mind works)

creaks and confuses
top branches that had just

begun to show buds
So the world becomes harder

once more
and to remember the trick

of foresight
once more becomes

the trick itself
a stubborn gathering of all

that is desired and not desired
stubbornly

as fibres of crocus
clutch each other while snow

rises along the back fence
My soul is black and

blacker by turns
as snow and wind and branches

out brutalize each other
I wait for the sharp crack and

plunge through hydro wires
So the world becomes all

that words and blossoms can
not make it

I retain the hope of
thin branches

in this last breathless
naming of weapons

Moving

---

for Anne

Snow had buried the leaves on St. Germain
Each morning we lifted our hands from pockets
into our dream of air

                         We believed this,
both of us, as if we had forgotten how to live
in just one body   The sound of bells

down a block of tattered, red trees was a word
for all the houses we will live in:
the shapelessness of light

We touched each other near the eyes
Everywhere we are
                         is a fresh track of an arriving heart

Fruit Cellar Poems

---

i

It's earthy here
What other word can I use?

I am underground, surrounded
by implements: typewriter, table,
pen, paper   I am waiting
for dankness to seep into me
First it makes the skin
smooth and clammy like the
belly of a fish Then descends
through the epidermis and dermis,
flesh and bone to marrow

I cannot be a beast here
I have quick visions of
vegetables with minds, Yonge Street
crowded with peaches in
Holt Renfrew dresses I take
up my pen deliberately
and carve these words into
processed pulp when the
mood is on me, when
I think I am light
shining out of the earth

ii

small windows
at ground level
allow my only

daylight here,
let me see the dust
and shelves lined with
preserves, squat jars
labeled and dated

After dark when I
cannot work here,
the jars hold this
cellar's only life:
the certainty of a
brief taste of peach
in February

And in spring, in
Longer daylight
I glance up from a page
and see entangled stems of roses —

I reach forward
in this chair, put my
finger to the screen and
rub the green, hardening
thorns until I draw one
drop of my blood, open
a small place in my body
for the spirit to forsake or
enter me

iii

Sometimes I feel these walls
around me
They are polite, always keep
their distance This one stays
an arm's length in front,

the others there and there
allowing me space

As I walk I can see
the darkness in corners,
this queer light that
conjures a graveyard:
dusk, after rain
a flushed sickle moon
like a slit in the sky

This table is a cheap
headstone, my words
epitaphs of feelings
I will take with me

iv

A storm coming, clouds
appear behind houses
It is the stillness before wind
Down here memory
is a cornered beast
It can be hart or hare
boar or wolf, no matter
There is never an open field

Slowly the cellar fills
with old words and feelings
the tired ghosts of images
In the rising wind, the
muted light, my elegies
begin to lack consolation

I form an aesthetic for descent:
heat lightning, the mind

a hunter cloud

v

Glance up from the page again
and see more than roses —
the trunk of the dying
Japanese cherry on the lawn

I heap curses on corroded pipes
swarthy, bare-chested plumbers
who swung muddy axes down
through wood into earth
Now roots suck up nothing

But my heart still beats
My fingers on these keys
chop out an elegy for leaves
the afternoon sun once turned
to burnished copper

vi

I come here to be closed in
And to open   This time
Rain stopped an hour ago
Now the smell of wet roses

In such air my memory
always goes to ballads:
the man with a face cut
from marble; the girl
with auburn hair and buried
in a flowering hill   The
words heart and abbey

dominate and refrain

A melody cracks
these concrete walls Soon
I believe I am wings and dust
My cells die and regenerate
without warning

4

Trying To Dream For My Son
(1984)

Elegy: Sometimes the Green Images

Rain all day
The Complete Piano Works of Grieg
gone through

Sometimes all I can see
is first snow on the garden chair
my grandfather built at eighty

or great uncle Walt dragging
a red canoe to shore
his footprints in wet sand
a string of perch on the grass

Late March brings its images:
half-light, a scherzo of birds,
a pewter tea-set on the mantle
dull as low cloud

Uncle Walt slit the perch bellies
at a table my eyes could
just see over   I watched
his careful scraping of gut
extraction of the delicate spine;
later carried them in newspaper,
proudly let them spill out
on the compost heap for the garden

Water rushes in sewer drains
High in a bare poplar
three crows balance their fat
black bodies on branches thinner
than their legs The street
becomes a mood of brown grass

Christmas 1972   My grandfather
ate oranges on the floor, his wife
upstairs with pins in her hip

called him by their son's name
There was no snow   I spent
the two dollars in my card
on cigarettes and shoelaces

Now, evening comes early
and with a new storm I sit
quietly with a glass
of recorked wine   Rain
from bare, thin branches drips
sotto voce on the drenched lawn

Singing Across the Ninth Concession

(Welland County; for Anne)

All week we have waited for rain,
the peninsula burning as if it did not have
water on three sides

Now we drive across it on a road straight
as a common fact, and the clouds
appear between windbreaks of poplars
like a person at a window

For an hour now I have heard grace notes
at the back of your voice
and remembered how our bodies change shape
at each anniversary

The ploughland darkens
Look, the wind is taking the earth
up out of the cornfield …

At McCabe's Fruit Stand we drive into the rain
and stick hands, arms, faces out of windows

For miles your drenched hair,
ground fog
the song we are singing back to the city:

a round with three verses,
beat, beat out to windshield wipers,
our voices intertwined like the top
branches of windbreaks, the field birds gurgling
up there under tough, veined backs of leaves

On the Headland

Dawn pulls mist from the lake
We sit with the fingers of four separate hands
Uncurling south-east

In this light for the first time I can see
You have a scar on your arm the shape of an easel

Which dry leaf will the wind choose
as partner?   Which hard bud will be the first
to soften and break on this branch
after five more months of words?

Birds fly uphill from the river:
in each wing there is a heart of light

We say things now: ice, ice
Our hands move at angles
like the memory of a body

For miles around men break the stems of corn

On our fingers we count places
The world will end
We do not begin with this one

Reading Plath by the Fountain
at Eaton Center: February

(for Anne)

Here only the old men are silent
Thrust by the corner-driven wind
into this sanctuary of light
and warm, they hunch
over canopied tables
occasionally lift a paper bag
from between their thighs
to swig from the twisted neck
They are out of fashion, their clothes
crumpled by the neon and the grit
Theirs is the silence of wizened friends,
certain, irascible: as if
for this camaraderie in the dream
of print dresses and young touches,
no words, now or then,
are better than the dream

Anne and I sit on the fountain's rim
She reads aloud from a Plath
she has been looking for, for years
and I, too, drop easily
into that silence listening hears
And when the fountain gurgles,
erupts suddenly a foot high
then surges up beyond the eyes
of the children on the balcony,
I do not wonder that souls may rise
without hope, or that,
like horizons or a dream of return,
promises dissolve again and then again

I listen for a silence in her words
I know ocean, cliff, the noise
of water finally reaching land

Carillon Over Stratford / Rain in October

What I may see
or taste in the raw air
is not important

I am only the cold water
in lakes
sometimes a wet, brown leaf
stuck to a curb

Sometimes I have no senses
but a need for light
an admiration for colour

The sound of the bells on the red trees
in the throats of swans

is the knell of grey air I feel
in the corners of houses
I have moved from

What I choose to touch
are broken twigs
the cold water

I inhale deeply
the smell of bright leaves on the islands
there are no bridges to

Trying To Dream for My Son

(for Tom)

It has been years since I dreamed of love
the old kind
like flowers
the one when a moment of eyes
hands, bodies meeting
freezes the hands of clocks
all over the world
forever

In the year my son is five
there is only the dream
of tall men with spindly legs
stick-men
with deformed chests
oblong heads
their eyes like caves, labyrinths
of missing limbs, memory and
veins spurting blood like fountains
They sprinkle salt in each other's wounds
and shove their fists in
They cry like birds under the horizon
carry scales
and lightning bolts
pray to the One who does not
kill without good reason
They are ugly
They will not disappear
They disease my old dream of love
Before I wake up my son comes home
with running sores on his wrists

What do I tell him
When do I tell him flowers
close themselves against the dark,
leaves turn their rough, veined backs
against wind and rain
When do I teach him to read
headlines, tell him there really are
tigers under the bed

What are the words to say his father's dreams,
this one of spindly men,
and the others that are all black, red,
purple on a white canvas
How long can I lie
How long until I can tell him the world
can be like a fresh cut on his hand

It is said the soul rises out of the body
dancing on invisible, perfect feet,
coughing dust out of its invisible throat,
dreaming of a skeleton with a heart
that trusts sunsets
and the eyes of man and beast all
with the same implacable love

Is this the heart that is growing in his body,
a defenseless one,
one born in a dream
like the old kind of love,
like the idea of a son with all
the angels of innocence
perfect
austere
having nothing to do with the earth
left him away from me out
into the world?

5

Northern Poems:
Where The Heart Catches Its Breath
(1986)

Katherine Cove

Turning   the car gently through a curve
and you are suddenly white letters on a green background,
a body of water hidden in the white pines

Down mud road   under green canopy
with the several flutes of the air
rehearsing a tune the way a blind man listens

for a change in the weather — the cove is
cold blue water   an osprey launched
for my eyes only   I kill the engine

and in the moment after the last, rough stutter
see you clearly: your hair was this light
your hands on the table in the blue kitchen

sometimes   the wings that close here after dark,
or the footprints of the animal that drank
in the silence until the flutes began playing …

Algoma Suite

Eight Ways of Listening to the Heart Catch its Breath

1

I am discovering the names for this place
Each one becomes a word   a shape
created by the muscles in my throat

At the curve inAnglican Church Road
my name on a mailbox   wild daisies

growing out onto the road. The house
is invisible behind blue spruce

and the bay   beyond thatgenerously
lifting the sound of its waves into the air

2

I have not walked here enough to know landmarks
when I see them. Each valley and hill
I enter between cliffs of pink granite,

or lava that is a dark red I did not think
could be. I do this blindly, on
faith the land will right itself. I do not hope
to recognize a tree, a curve in the road, a village …

So far,   I can say only this: a cliff
is an enormous silence   and a sudden view of the lake
the heart remembering how to listen to your voice

3

The Charles Hibbard at its peace out there in the bay,
Its logs copper salt pork   long
Dispersed   is severe invisible history

To touch it   I can only dip my hand
into the bay   be surprised at the stealth

of a wave when it rolls over my elbow …
My wet arm dries quickly in the wind

And then, at Agawa Rock, I brace myself on
slippery granite   trace the shape of a canoe
four suns   a giant horse try to look

straight up the cliff into the sky without
giving in to the body that wants to tip

in slow motion over into the lake …
My head is full of the wind. The whitecaps
tell their story in a language I can see

4

I am a history of looking for this place
And now here, there is a memory
of dark rooms and rain   the way

a language of this place formed itself
out of a moment near a window   an awkward
dive into a lake when I was ten

From the window I saw light begin
downstream   the darkness of an island
become shapes. And that dive:

the water taking my body without question,
my lungs listening to a new story of my breath

5

This is one more place the whole body can hear
There is a sound of wind come
down miles of pine forest   or through the angle

a cliff makes in the air. I think it is
the muscles that listen best   contract
in silence   expand when the language of waves

brings its white messages to the cliffs …
I do not think about what I am hearing
except to know the silence of my own body

and that there is a word, maybe two,
I will be dreaming one night when the wind
sounds like this   or when rain

on a sturdy roof wakes me, suddenly,
sits me up in the darkness full of listening

6

I send my words over this land in search
of what memory grows into. Even one story

to celebrate absence of rain on the hairpin
curve above Batchawana Bay … To find a voice

for the 'Ava Maria' scratched into rockface
near Theano, above the point of rocks

that creeps out into the lake. The island
glowing in a hand of bright water   is

Ossifrage, named after the freighter. I have
read guidebooks: can not discover for how many

men these cliffs were the last sight of land …
My heart becomes too big. I think I can hear words
in hard maples   angles of rock. The story
and its voice living here like a child

who talks to strangers.

7

Queen Lady's Slipper Bunchberry
Marsh marigold   Trillium

Some of my days have lived like cut flowers
in a jar. A knowledge of bright colour
waiting patiently. Even the small

refraction that tricks the eye just
below the surface   (that one more reason

to look everywhere). I am alive here in
this place where light grows in a swamp,

where some people are like a clear morning,
and some the colour dusk can be if

there is rain. Heat   fills the air with
that one smell of the earth   the swamp
growing inside itself the way one breath
prepares the body for another … I send

the part of me that believes in every memory
on a walk to the far shore of blue spruce:

It makes it   and will think of this marsh,
the invisible water, one day when the world
is just air   an empty sleeve   or waiting

8

Sometimes a lake   is the words I think of
when I see your hand on a pillow. Those sounds
I keep behind my eyes and call to

often. And sometimes I have seen a lake
become all the colours that are hidden in light:
those evenings I sat alone in a white chair

and felt my eyes open and open … Or there is
the lake that welcomes rain into its body
as if it were a language it had

forgotten. This one   Superior   is not
words. The blue   the pale distance   or the sound
of dark waves reaching for the top of a cliff:
so far beneath speech I think I am walking
on the safe rim of a heart

Sault Ste. Marie

6

The Revels
(1986)

Along Benson Creek

This August is like a woman
Who gets men without moving

                       Robert Lowell

1

Now that each step takes my body
past beech trees in their sheaths of metal
& the heart winds like a heron over drowned land
looking & waiting
its one & one & one
cadence of great wings —

& now that all the animals
are hypnotized by sunlight
& the cells in their humming, dark brains
bloat & scar
so each memory of shelter   a cool place
to breathe & breathe & be still
is a thing tossed up in the wind   a cut root —

my own dark eyes are bowing to bits of fur,
a half-skeleton of trout

A gray rock burns my palm
When I step into the arm of the river
it is as if I could make that great,
fleshy pitch into the air

& the island will catch me

2

Day by day the sun in its elaborate breathing
steals green from the hill
A search for water becomes
a search for the origin of your name

You stand here as if your one body
is the only thing moving
& listen to the sluice of blood through your arm —

the division & division of your cells,
a pattern of light on running water

If you stand here long enough you can hear
rust flake in your bones …

In the grass, spiders shrink on their webs
like bits of fruit
Even Blue Devilweed fades …

The hill becomes a place of snakeskins,
curled   brittle
One touch dissolves them

3

Stillness   heat   tigerlilies
This is how you touch your wife's body

How severe history can be
Your mind like a rock that is never pulled out of water,
a breeding ground for unintelligible speech,
nosed by fish dreaming
of wooden boats   clear bodies

being an island …

You   and the blue heron
You fear   something alive   caught in your throat
a knot in the muscles while flying

Silence   shallow water pattern of light
You believe how you love
is the only creature with a voice

This voice
Skin   brain   heart   wanting

Beach Stones

(for Tom and Anne)

1

The smooth, coloured stones
my son picked out of the beach
with his eager eye and careful
index finger and thumb

and now sealed in a jar of water

are not the eyes of the earth I imagine them
The jar and the water with their message
of how clearly light clings to the shape
of each object under the sun

that is just one more inaudible voice

2

Or are they eggs pushed up by the earth
where everything grows

My son wants to plant the only brown
& purple-speckled one in the garden

A fun tree, he says,
purple for lilac in May

so I imagine the hard particles
dissolve & see

the colours of a forest I can hold

just now, in my hand

3

Each of the bodies I live in
Has a different shape
and each soul a colour
it has brought in from the light:

purple, brown, the one clean
white that shines out of the sun,
and black, and yellow,
the orange where a match is lit …

My son with his mother's clear eyes
rubs a wet, green stone on my arm

colouring me
his picture of a man

4

The three of us now, in the water
with me skipping flat, brown stones
and counting them
two, up to nine
Three more steps and we would swim
and he drown

Think of the light way she holds him
and of our eyes floating at the front of the brain

between the shore and open water
where the earth, invisibly, falls away

and the stones, those dark, wet
eyes I hum through the air

twist their way down through the current
and stop moving

and wait

Van Gogh With His Eye On A Bird

1

Is not a man
and not a bird   Paint from imagination, said Gauguin
That meant, Don't look   or Look closely

Under low cloud   in mist his whole body
humming its C
above high C

and then, in low avenues, a street is a colour that is not
its colour: green metal, yellow lanes, the flower you
want to live in   Its wings are oleander leaves touching
a blue and white vase …

This picture is always there   at the front of his eyes
A still membrane

The light always changing

2

Yellow paint is a way of saying what is possible   Sometimes
I use it to tell the severe history of things made of water,
down here, among slow feet and colour that blooms
                                        in the throat

At night everything is still   That is the illusion the birds
want me to believe, tucked away in their nests, always
watching me   So I take a brush of yellow from the messy
colour box and twirl it across the sky,
                                        or paint a painting

of a room that says: *Look how I live inside the sun There are all these colours moving, being moved*

My hands and my eyes and my muscles are language
                                    I cannot control
They are the wind down here where I live

3

Breath and a breath   and a colour
is the rhythm of a bird high over a field
                                    The baffling pitch
and rise, in which no muscle moves, is whoosh,
                                    and spin,
and the small brain collapsed in on itself He is only one
of the men listening for heartbeats   the wings of the
body in their hiding place …

Up there, the underbellies of clouds are red before the
sun climbs   later, like a tipped colour box   and then,
the birds come with all their messages to dip and soar
inside the light …

Search for a bird in his paintings   Each one is dabbed far
back in the sky   Where you put a heart
for safekeeping

Open Winter

(Digging in God's Country)

Digging in God's country,
the heart in its small contortions
believes this, that …

And sometimes in the evening
it skims the surface of the lake

                    dips

in cold water and lifts
off again

I walk here with my heart like a cipher
The thrill of a cardinal in a bare black maple
that cantata
that answers to the wind
turns the muscles in my body to water

Lake Simcoe with its heart
of black water in November
How will I keep this
inside me

Like a gravestone inscribed
'Death interrupts all that is mortal'
Like a man who can see
birds under the horizon

A crow
is the colour of a meadow
after fire

You do not imagine
red under the feathers
the blue veins behind the eyes

You say the heart, like the bird,
is a black knot of muscle
on a fencepost, the wild

miniature daisies
still open in the cold air
a foil … To dream

a universe of plants
in Georgina Township
is to leave no room for that

yellow spike of a beak
Through the cold light
at the edge of a field,

the shadow of a crow carrying
something by the tail
A second later, marsh-hawk

screeching   They go
and the silence is
white petals

Black River
where you begin
in me
is a place my heart
abandoned

As a child I toyed
with you   crushed
crabs in my fist like so
many brown leaves   shattered
your glass dome of water
with mottled stones …

Now your land knows
nothing of itself   how it
sags in weak sunlight
like an old barn

or a man who has walked
miles into the wind
would stand before a fire

I still listen to your music
The notes come to me
one at a time drops
of water on my hand
beading   running together

What a man listens for   is a voice

rain   a black sluice
in the brown fields

a sudden squall   that changes the air

          There are days for walking miles
          in the long gray valley of Pefferlaw River
          where water is the colour of stone

          He gets his feet wet
          His knees learn the angles of walking

Embankment, smooth boulder, gravel …

The only voice
is the one of evening

when a film of ice grows
at the edge of the river

In it are black dull eyes:
islands   hurt things

on the way home

At midnight when there are no voices
you can not tell the sky from the lake

This is the time you discover
what you can do

How you sit at a table alone
without muscles

with the whole world quiet
and not moving:

a sleeping hand

And this is when you think there once
was a bird that flew so long

it could not remember branches
It listened only to silence

It went blind …

Down to the shore in bare feet
You can do this

You slide your hands into the lake:
fish jump near the far shore …

November   The lake
talks all night of summer bodies:
clean flesh   the eyes
of young trout …

What is dying all over
Georgina Township
is the clamber of a heart
that once listened closely

Now the songbirds are all
things I am trying to remember
They are changing themselves
They did not want me

to go with them   Listen:
a man is watching the moon
The lake cries under the wind

The men in the Anchor Bar manoeuvre their stomachs up to
the round tables   Each man sits with his back   straight
His round shoulders are rock Buttons stretch white
thread exposing navel, hair, white skin   Shirt sleeves
rolled tight at the bicep

I am the thin man here   The one who can't talk easily of
knives   I wince when I cut into the belly of smallmouth or

trout, or back a hook out of an eyeball
On the wall, above labels of species, weight, and
fishermen, fish gleam in the orange light   Each of
their mouths open, as if frozen an inch from the hook

I come to this place to watch the mouths of men   Beer foam
on the upper lip   And I listen to their voices, the
deep voice in the shallows off Thorah Island   The
smallmouth there in the reeds are energy, the throat of
the world   Swimming toward these men as long as they
live

Like the heart aging
Like a lover walking into the room
Like the texture of flowers
Like dusk
Like the graveyard where your father is buried
Like listening to a clock
Like your wife's eyes in the dark

the first snow at mid-morning

You are the one sitting at the window
You are the one warming his hands at a coffee cup
You are the one making first tracks down to the lake
All that snow dissolving
like promises like words on the tongue

All day I watch light
bringing its ways of seeing to the earth

A man was once a child
He imagines   he saw everything

Now   sparrows
are shadows that want to be light

He stands still opens & closes his eyes

He wants to see it happen

The sparrows are never where
he remembers them

A December night   a low fire
A lantern

The signal
is a loud buzz of insects
on a summer afternoon

Or is it only
a fox scratching a tree

without a voice   to promise anything?

In this place what a man thinks of women
is not true

Each has large eyes
is dreamed white skin
how you listen to water

There is a distance between their hands
and the transparent skin of your chest

Touch
is like searching for a name
an approach of birds

How a man waits for the dark sky
that slow dance

alone
with birdsong
with
his own breath
making clouds in the white air …

Black and white water
under rough cloud
As if the lake could boil …
On Jackson's Point the fish huts
are bright statues
Their locks bang in the wind

In the slow channel between
Georgina Island and Royal Beach,
two men pull up a gill net

A tangle of trout and whitefish
Ooze of roe   a million
cut orange eyes

I live here like a brave man
I hold my wrists up to the wind
I talk to strangers

In late afternoon you are listening to trees crack in the

cold light   Birch, elm, the sugar maples
in their glaze of frost

This winter you are a thin branch   You greet the wind, a
carnivore when it comes straight down the lake
At night,
it is the sound of the other side of the moon …

There are so many trees here, you cannot tell which ones
crack in the cold light   You close your eyes
                                        and imagine
your body splintering The warm hemorrhage
You were dreaming of trees   Now you shiver
                                        in gray light
Once upon a time there was a sound everyone knew
They said they wanted to hear it   They said the trees bow
down their heads   Relax your shoulder now   Listen
It
is so still you can believe the wind is dead

A black dog wanders in a frozen field

You would think the heart
had given up   that edges
of frozen grass cut into rough paws,
or a bell   tied to its neck

echoed there the windbreaks
curving the sound so
the dog surrounds itself

Late January   sky the blue
of faint memory   Absence
is a creature you can touch

Blame the glass wings of the heart
or the wind in furrows that is
a breath caught in the earth

The black dog The open field
A piece of glass out there
waiting for a foot   waiting for spring

A weekend of snow   and then

at dawn, near Sibbald,
only wind

In this place my lantern
gutters recovers

On the window, breath
Melts a peep-hole

The silent eye put to it
waters   sees

blackbirds, one jay
gripped to thin branches and the road
not plowed

All over Georgina Township small animals
cower
without blankets   fire

We are waiting for footprints
a sound that is not the wind

How this country makes a man dream
of rock and ice,
of trees rooted
one hundred miles in the earth

a sound behind a shed past midnight
is the only sound in the world

The air is a giant bell
A small cloud of breath
catches in the throat

Shards of ice
melt on the back of the hand

— a voice dissolving in an open field

— a man remembering a time when he was loved

Sometimes I think the whole night
is a heart beating in the sky

Shards of light
A candle fluttering in the voice

Georgina Township on a clear day
in winter
is a star escaping from a dead
planet
the beating of a heart that wants
to live longer than anything
else alive

Between the thumb and the finger
there is space for something to live

The sparrows are men who remember everything

Out of bare trees they fly up into the light

What do I make of a man
who walks on the rim of the lake
looking up at stars
getting dizzy
taking a toe-hold on the cliff

His heart is a blue thing
opening in the night air
His fingers   points of light
The words he breaks in his mouth
are *wall*   *sky*   *window*

There is a silence
between the veins in his chest
and the cold skin   Inside,

young trout move slowly
as a current far inland

Ground is broken
Light   gathers itself
Everything is white   & raw   & half-blind

Far out at the edge of the marsh-hawk's wing:
a slice like a wound
vibrating

A man thinks about the age of the earth
In another life it was a man
watching birds

North wind at Leacock's grave:

The cocked heads of starlings,
their legs   bits of wire straightened
up on a branch
                        They take all this in,
open their beaks and gulp down the wind
again and again

A man comes to this place believing only water
or machines
or a tug of earth beside a mountain
can move rock
Now wind shoves the moss on a boulder south
and the eye sees rock twitch …

This gift of seeing one more thing
at its new angle

Traces of snow frozen at the base
of headstones: a brief mortar

Wind gathers the starlings up to the steeple
of Susan Sibbald's church —

they open their mouths again
and from under the lake
and the weight of more than a century she has gone
without praying,
she pricks up her ears

Are those echoes rising through the shallow frost?

The way a man hears music in the distance
and rehearses each melody he knows …

A serenade   a flute
warming to a mouth

March   Black River, rising

I stand still in the damp heart
of Georgina Township

and breathe and breathe the sunlight

The songbirds' voices catch in small bones of the ear
a stream trickling into the lake
                              The first moments of rain
in the fields …

You can walk now as slowly as a man in summer   With
loose hands, and the muscles
in your shoulders part of the air
You can forget your name, you can make
handprints on the beach and say they are the tracks
of some extinct, young animal that stood here once, rooting
for moss under the bushes   Dust in your eyes for the first
time this year

After months of walking in soggy fields, you come to
your senses like a man who wakes up in the middle
of the night and listens to rain   A language for one

night of the year   The songbirds in the dark   Each eye
without a lid
Each throat tuning

I wrap my body   in night air
smell of grass turning brown to green
a wet smell   a slow river
a man discovers what he can do
Skin   & water   & air
His whole body   a road   an open field
Or traveling there

7

The White City Poems
(1985-1986)

Colours & Walking

In my white city every colour lives deep in itself
the way breath lives inside air.   You make your choice
and try to hold it in your arms

There is a way of walking that has nothing to do with balance
Even the light-hearted body stumbles

and sound, like wind on a night deep in winter, comes
from all directions at once.   My body is learning

the given names of the world by heart, and the past
is something the skin remembers best. This is the
white city within the heart.

Everything here lives in the open air   surrounded
by colour: that bright raincoat

pale nipple   the way my hands gently
touch what they touch in the dark or the light

Green & White

Listen
Tom has said, "The book about crack-up"

Tom & David have written every poem
about seagulls over the magic water
of their own white city — white motion on white…

I've lived there.   Heard a blonde woman sleeping
An Irish poet break a bottle against a wall

Limestone and late evening light
is the tune my skin learned to sing

take me by the hand. That is how it feels to touch
a city where everything is a colour of stone,
a pastel watercolour where birds are the only

thing moving. No, there was my body, its heart
tangled on my sleeve, singing at the top of its voice

— the sound of gulls on Johnson Street that morning
in October when your eyes were everywhere I looked…

Hear it? Your room back there with its silence
the blue curtains drawn back.   What we whispered

dissolving there as the sounds make their way
like magic through the white air

Learning to think

in the white city about strippers' black spiked heels,
flat bellies, rainbow tattoo above the right breast

about sounds in the beige wall after dark — how they
scuttle the way a man does on an icy sidewalk, the man
and the sound keeping the awkward rhythm of their bodies

about the way each time I listen to traffic surge
from a green light I wonder about the shape the heart
takes on coming into love

or there is the way a woman's spine bends under
the weight of one more pregnancy — this last one,
she says, all the little bottles and brushes
under the make-up mirror go
unused for days

about the shape each word gives to the mouth
say, tonight near a low blue candle, or tomorrow
when dusk will come again and the sunset make its way
gloriously down St Clair West

or there is the way light wanders through the body
when I cut myself shaving

the way a man and a woman try to live down their marriage
the way your belly feels against the belly of your lover

the way a man sits in a doorway, high summer, his clothes
thirty years out of fashion and his body the texture
of a coin you find on the sidewalk.

And listen: you can hear the brain turning its blind corners,
the heart feeling its way through love

the invisible nerve-ends that open their warm arms up
wide for you

New Words

This is the poem about language I am writing,
the old words for the old deeds for the old flag
have dissolved in my throat & are gone

Here is one word: lover's hand.   And another:
our talk of a red car that takes us to another city

Speak these words slowly, let sound touch sound
the way a man dreams what he wants to happen

and write an elegy for the old deeds, capture the soft voice
and measured tones of a heart hiding in the body

Then: the new poem.   The sound of a mouth around words,
the melody of dark air that fills the park we walk through
                                        bravely,
at midnight, the word 'lover's hand' between us,

a hieroglyphic, the picture I make in this poem,
the sound my throat wraps its warm muscles around

Black

The slow advent of right words
when thin winter light and sheer curtains marry
Even the green pillow,
or dusty Gibbard end table my parents
saved for in 1943 — even these things,
or especially these things mumble in the beige corners
where shadow seems to grow from the floor…

This is black, the other colour of the city
You'd think the heart would stop watching
You'd think everybody was a pane of glass
smudged on both side

I live here   take antibiotics with my coffee,
Remember that black is the absence of colour,
& live for the moment energy becomes clear
As it can/   when I hear the sounds under my skin,
Those voices that keep on talking and can't
get out of the dark.   You can touch me,
have at your fingertips the modulation,
inflection/   tone of me, this dark

that grows inside all this light, the short breaths it takes
behind sheer curtains, each word that is wrong
for now keeps waiting —

I think it is the way skin waits for water,
the cells flake and grow and even light,
the naked eye, won't let you see it happen

Construction

My white city is made up of small pink nipples,
orange garter belt   gold ankle bracelet
Its streets are the way your mouth finds mine in the dark

Look at this: the sunset is a dream I had
of how I would touch your body.   The streetlamps
along St. Clair West light up suddenly
as far as we can see…

I know there are plants growing just under my skin:
each one is green & tall & wants to brush against you
I live this way now. The long story of my childhood

the first morning I woke to find a blonde hair tangled in
powder-blue sheets — they are songs, now, I sing by heart
Let each song I have learned be a place on my body

you will touch.   This is the white city I am making.
You lie beside me as we watch all the light in the world
stream through sheer curtains.

If I close my eyes I can see violet, red, yellow
move slowly as my fingers do on your back. We are
living this way. The white city & our bodies in one place

The city and our bodies feel their way into a dark room
where sound is their lover breathing…

Alcohol

This is a way of seeing my body move
away from its edges.   The angles
I live inside, as if you hugged me,
disappear

The broken bottle in the Irish poet's room
The wall stained with beer and bristling
invisible shards of brown glass

Or Jim's boat with the sails down
set off to invade Wolfe Island past midnight
the five of us pissing into the lake from starboard

Remember those times as you kiss my chest
If I close my eyes I can feel only your skin,
The flickering of each nerve in the pattern
you trace without thinking

I'm thinking of arson, white ash glowing
on the crossbeams, loving my life away,
the shovelsful of debris I heave with my big shoulders

all over the city with you, as we drink and the candle
flicks light across the bed, as I am not myself,
the texture of my skin that of water with a voice,

but no ear, that sings its prayers out loud,
weightless, and unafraid, knowing the words

Breathing

When you are asleep I cannot think only of you
This cramped third floor is full of angles I must learn

I imagine the pores of my body close in the cold air,
or my knee split on a corner of the toy box
if I stood up now to listen to your children breathing

Would I smooth the jumble of blankets?
Would I reach into the crib with my cold arms
and pick up your daughter as I have my son,
so light, that small breath warm on my shoulders?

I see the ghost of my body slide back under the sheets
You haven't moved. The westbound streetcar
shakes the window again as my body warms & my eyes

melt inside it like ice. I'm asleep. I'm here,
part of the breathing in your room's dark air
The air you have listened to for the silence
of a man not talking.

White flowers on the blue quilt
Shine like your hand in the dark

Dreams

Dream this, said the colour blue:
A river on its way through a landscape
you make up with your own words —
rockface and meadow here, factory
and yellow water there — and when you
recognize the place it is an expression
of the wings your body has, some days,
the wings that catch air in their perfect construction
and lift you into the next life again and again…

And dream this, said red:
The woman in the red sweater who laughs behind
each barrier, who listens as if her ears
can hear the other side of the world.   A name
on cracked lips in winter, her arms buried in wool
In the snow, at a distance inside the eye where
a casement window stands open in December — think of it,
where the cold air from the moors enters the room, is
breathed in, the blood waiting for it, opening a vein…

Or tallow, dreams this:
Southwestern Ontario in full voice,
sideroads, miles of vegetables and childhood
to come back to.   As if the one word
the mouth learns to say properly in each life
hides behind a door to a chamber of the heart
until the mouth is ready — one day in high summer,
the golden canoes on the lake wrapping themselves in
                                        silence

listening can hear…

These colours that dream about themselves,
the names they were born with,
can't help singing,

a vein that sticks out on the temple,
you look at/ and look at/ until you can't see it

Listening to Buddy Holly: 1 February 1986

I listen to Buddy Holly not fade away as the snow
changes to rain and a streetlight
blinks, ice melts on the window, the phone

rings and its you with the voice I remember
close to my ear in the dark.   I hear you in the black
receiver, in the other ear a story about

"the day that I'll die" over primitive
rhythm guitar.   The two voices sing
a counterpoint of different rooms, different

light I have opened my eyes to.   What
did you say?   The words wander in my body
like a slow river, a memory of your lips

on my shoulder as I sit quietly beside a lamp.
Is this the night we have been afraid of for months,
the one night the two of us dream of airplanes,

a field crusted with snow, our bodies
in different light singing out loud
words by heart, words, oh boy, we remember

so easy, before the heart went down

Untitled

Rain begins in the night
          an open window   no screen

The nightmare I wake from
is my body in a bed without you:
you become space   my arms flop into

my whole body wired for sound…

This room is one of many places
to learn how to speak unnoticed,
to be as breathless as rain…

The sound of trees in rough air
puts words in my mouth,
sound in my ear   invisible
as black things in the dark

Breathing is only one thing to do with the air…

There are old dances I light a match to:
your breathing: nights like this
          the billow of a white curtain
as you close the window   almost…

Space beside me is never a silence,
you words   you movement of air,
you blind step from bed
to window…

Smoke/Fire

I live beside your body on the night I say
there is no future. The words burn in my throat,
make a cancer. You say you taste smoke

Watch my tongue as it moves, kitty-corner,
across your belly. In candlelight
the line of spit shines like a web in rain.
I'm the spider. I eat the air above your skin.

One night I argued with this room.
I told it everything I know & it said
nothing for an hour

Look: it has no eyes
If it had a mouth I would live in constant danger
It has no blood, only dust and corners
If it had skin I could put my body against it

I look for a flicker in the eyes of my friends
blue   brown   grey   green
The colours of the fire I spend my time with

But there's no future. You heard me say this
when your hand started to move over my chest
I said it so quietly, a wisp of smoke in your hair

I am alive beside you. Everything is burning.
The night. My throat. Both halves of the brain.
This fever that lives out its life
breath by breath, beside you, not beside you

Not said, the tears when Robert went missing, but this can be said…

by Cathy Ford, Poet/Fictioniste

Robert Billings and I found ourselves aligned several times over the course of a few years, in meeting as members of the League of Canadian Poets, and considering many artistic, political, and cultural issues in common. When I actually contemplated standing for election to serve as the LCP President, I first asked Robert and Fred Cogswell, to stand together as Vice-Presidents. The LCP needed their wisdom, experience, forthrightness, fairmindedness, their mutual abilities to call mysteries for what they actually were, and I needed their support for the first President to emerge from the ground-breaking Feminist Caucus newly established in the LCP.

As a triumvirate, we signed all our executive correspondence together for months, and tackled a crippling deficit, rescued the writer's direct support programs which had been jeopardized, and helped the LCP find its foundation again. We moved from a thirty hour annual general meeting where the membership thrashed out the fact that the LCP was rather out of touch with its own business, to the place where as an organization, we remodeled and reconfirmed our commitment to a community of poets working together to assert rights, recompense, and representation of Canadian poetry, in Canada, and internationally.

None of this could have been done without Robert Billings, who was the one of the three of us in Toronto, the one who could reach B.C. and New Brunswick, and the regional representatives spread across the country, with his sheer brainpower, his careful assessment of an ongoing crisis situation, and his firm resolve, with Fred and myself, to help the LCP save itself. I was also, during this executive year, glorying in my first pregnancy, and the birth of my son. I can still hear Robert's compassionate, sardonic, humour-filled voice over the phone, long-distance, and his hands-on help in every aspect of the day-to-day business of the LCP when we had to take over the administration of the offices in Toronto and go begging to every one of our granting agencies for renewed and forgiving support.

I will always remember Robert saying to me: "I remember this", when he picked up my son in his straw basket, four months, still nursing, when our little family flew to Toronto so Robert and Fred and I could chair the AGM in June 1986, and deliver our new executive director, Angela Rebeiro, to bring us all into the present. I have given thought many times to the work Robert did for the League, how much he suffered wanting a life partner, wanted to trust the world, wanted to not miss a day of his son's life, or give up on any of the critical and editorial work he was doing, while at the same time, never for a moment letting go of his own beautifully accomplished work.

Robert was genuinely hurt by the ruthless ambitions of others, the star-making system of Canadian letters that was beginning to glow, and hardened by the times he was "hit on" by those who thought they might make use of him to accomplish only their own intent or self-service. Innocently, but oh so accurately, he said to me once: "Some of them are sharks. Don't they know we are working for the community?" Robert and I knew and understood each other pretty well over a relatively short period of time, of necessity, and I have sincerely appreciated that over the years since, my personal regard second only to how much I admired his own poetics, and therefore, his published works.

The gratefulness I feel in finding the work of Robert Billings once again in hand, in print, with the "last poems" included is difficult to explain without tying personal to professional valuation. Robert's poetry was and is much more important than ever fully recognized, and his editorial expertise left a mark of conscientiousness and understanding of the work of other writers on every project or magazine he touched. Long overdue, this collection, thanks to Sharon Berg, brings wonderful clarity to all the darknesses and the light Robert wrestled with, his empathic eye, as well as his impatience, even defiance, facing down anything status quo.

Some of all of our dreams are here, including a reminder, a remembrance of a writer who "dead serious about life", gave service not only to his own work, but also to the writing community. "I am alive, I am naming my weapons", stated his intent and measured his sense of the artistic community, his own political relationship with the League of Canadian Poets, and his support of its feminist caucus and the changes precipitated during his years on the executive.

The colourations of his caring engagement with nature, his attention to silence, his picture making in the air, "the heart feeling its way through love" - all recording the haunting shadowed invisible — render these poems technically perfect landscapes fully Canadian, brilliant with birdsong, unavoided grief, urgency, compelling intelligence and, in his writing life's work, hard won grace.

Epilogue

by Sharon Berg

The title of this book comes from one of Robert's final poems, one that he wrote to me. How to explain that I was the one who ended up holding onto a sheaf of ten poems, typed by Robert and corrected in his own hand, when he passed over? These are part of a manuscript he was calling *The White City Poems*. That collection represents a different vein in his work and some of his finest writing. It is also the inspiration for this book, which begins by collecting poems selected from all of his other work as foreshadowing.

It was 1985 when Robert Billings and I first met. He had accepted an important poem of mine, a long piece called *Coming of Age*. He intended to include it in the next issue of *Poetry Canada Review* (PCR), a periodical that he edited. Nick Drumbolis, a Toronto-based rare book seller who was important to everyone's understanding of Canadian Literature for his analysis at that time, told me I didn't realize what I'd done in that poem. Now Robert said he thought it was important to the history of how Canadian writers would handle a difficult subject matter.

However, the piece was so long he asked me to meet him at his ground-floor apartment to discuss its layout in the Winter 1985/86 issue of PCR. As it turned out, it took up an entire page in the Review. It was during this meeting that Robert and I realized we were almost neighbours along the St. Clair West corridor in Toronto. I lived in a third-floor walk-up apartment, over stores, several streetcar stops away but still within walking distance.

Robert served me coffee as we talked about my poem and I asked about his work for PCR. We began to visit in the way that two ordinary people relate to one another. It is some 34 years ago now, so I can't remember who first suggested that we meet again, but we began dating very soon after that meeting. We got together every second or third day, most often at my home as I had two young daughters.

Robert was separated from his wife, though he often visited to see his son. I remember it was a very painful period for him. For one thing, Robert wasn't a man who was entirely comfortable living on his own. He desired a partner who understood him, not solitude. But he was also Vice-President of the *League of Canadian Poets* (LCP) and his work on the magazine and for the LCP kept him very busy. He needed someone who accepted him as a writer and understood the other demands upon him.

As for me, at the previous AGM for the LCP, I'd been convinced by Bronwen Wallace and Erin Mouré to become the Chair of *The Feminist Caucus*. I also had my own writing to fill in any moments when I was not tending to my children. In other words, Robert and I were both highly independent and busy people.

At one point, Robert and Greg Gatenby met to organize an event called the *World Poetry Festival* at Harbourfront. Members of the LCP had been asked to mail-in a slip of paper that offered their 1st, 2nd, and 3rd choices for someone to represent the LCP at this brand new festival. Robert and Greg met to count the votes together. On coming to my home from that meeting, Robert told me with some surprise, "You missed being voted to represent the League by one vote."

"I guess I should have voted for myself then," I quipped.

"You didn't?" he responded, shaking his head. "Oh, you're an idiot!"

"It's pretty unethical to vote for oneself when you're choosing the best author."

"Except that everyone does it," he returned.

"So who won?" I asked, thinking I knew. His answer indicated I'd guessed correctly.

"Margaret Atwood. You missed being the LCP Rep by one vote for Margaret Atwood." He shook his head again.

"Well, that only means we would have tied, doesn't it? Who would you have picked from a tie-vote?" This was bravado talking. I actually felt some-what dumbfounded that I'd come that close to being picked.

"We'd already decided it would be 'the new face'," was his response.

Looking back, the mid-1980s were a period of huge upheaval and shifting priorities in the world of Canadian letters and creative writing. In many ways, Robert and I were both at the tip of that wave though I didn't realize it for myself at the time. I was struggling to assert myself with a style of feminism that was resisted by several strong women poets in the LCP. I accepted interested men at our meetings, to talk to them rather than excluding them, while many of the men in the organization flatly resisted even a hint of feminism. Robert had positioned himself in such a way that he had a degree of influence through both his editorial and his analytical assessment of Canadian poetry. In fact, James Deahl, who recently released an anthology of Canadian poetry himself, suggests that Robert was so highly respected for his poetry, his criticism, and his sense of organization, that he most likely would have been elected as the next President of the LCP.

Yet, Robert and I rarely talked about the craft of writing, or even what other writers were doing, while we were together. We were comfortable with each other but neither assumed anything about the other person. We talked. There were few silences between us. Still, my two daughters, Ila and Brynna, occupied a lot of our focus. Of course, Robert also talked about his son, Tom, and how much he valued the time he spent with his boy. He shared many stories about Tom's interaction with other Canadian poets as he often took his son with him on trips to the LCP office. In fact, Robert took the unusual (at that time) position of being a stay-at-home father during his marriage. But he had concerns. He talked about his personal habits, though he rarely referred to any of his moods, telling me they were really strong.

"I always eat breakfast at the same restaurant, at the same time, sitting at the same table. I always order the same food. I've often thought that if I just changed my habits I would disappear."

Saying this didn't alarm me at the time, though I did think about what that meant — about how Robert saw himself as a man. I accepted that he was different from most other men I'd spent time with, but there was also something similar in him to what I knew from home. I'd not been raised in an ordinary household. The poem Robert accepted to PCR spoke to some of that difference. In addition, several family members had heightened my awareness and sensitivity to living with depression.

In addition, my older brother, a half-brother, was Al Purdy's son through my mother. This threw Brian and I into a different relationship with the world of literature than most authors in Canada have experienced. The fact that Brian was not publicly recognized as Al's son — though he did share pleasant visits with his father — was really hard on him. In fact, I witnessed times when people threw cruel challenges at him, telling him he was a fake and should change his name. He often fell into a dark funk as a result. In fact, I was raised with several family members who suffered from serious mood swings. Perhaps that's why I saw Robert's struggle to maintain his emotional and intellectual balance as normal. I'd grown up in that house, as it were.

I don't think it's only hindsight to say that Robert and I were good for each other. We were both shy and socially awkward. Though each of us engaged in demanding independent activities, we also had a strong respect for each other. In fact, at my home he was so easy-going it was fine for the TV to play cartoons for my children while we sat at the table in my kitchen and simply talked over coffee. Or we would pack a warm supper into a basket and walk to a local schoolyard for a picnic because there were so few parks in that neighborhood for my children to play in.

It was Halloween of 1985 when Robert took me to a 'black and white party' at Michael Ondaatje's home. We were definitely an item by then. My kids both adored him, and though I'd not even met Tom yet, we felt really comfortable with each other and the easy going relationship that we were developing.

At least, that was true… up until the moment he phoned me from the Emergency Department at a local Hospital. It was the 1st day of February 1986. He said he'd just been diagnosed with a disease that he had to speak to me about. I braced myself, thinking he'd tell me he had cancer due to his smoking, or that he had cirrhosis of the liver due to his drinking. But no, he said he had Thrush and his Doctor had told him it was a sexually transmitted disease. His next words thoroughly shocked me, but no more than what he said after that.

"Just admit you gave it to me, and I'll forgive you."

The problem was, first, that I knew I didn't have any symptoms. In fact, I didn't believe that I had Thrush myself. Plus, where would I have gotten it from?

"Just admit you slept with someone," he insisted. "The Doctor told me it's a sexually transmitted disease. I haven't been with anyone else, so that means that you were."

"No, that's not true," I insisted. Yet, he'd planted a seed of self-doubt. It had been almost two years since my previous relationship. Could I be a carrier for the disease and suffer no symptoms? I went to see my own Doctor and asked if I could carry Thrush and be unaware of it. He examined me, said that a) I was clear, and b) no, I couldn't *carry* a disease like Thrush. In fact, he suggested my boyfriend was accusing me to deflect from his own actions.

Later that evening, Robert phoned me again. There was no fight but when we hung up, we both felt raw. The next day, Robert sat at my kitchen table. He presented me with a small sheaf of poems, each one typed on a different sheet of paper, some with editorial corrections written in his own hand, all of them folded in half together. He said he wanted me to read them.

"That's some of my new work," he said, "from my *White City Poems*."

"Your new manuscript?"

"Very new."

In fact, the first several poems were dated Christmas day, 1985. The last was dated February 1st, 1986. I glanced at them, but I couldn't read them at the time. So I refolded them and set them to the side.

Robert was silent for a long moment. I realize now that these poems were his testament to me. Proof of his feelings. But we were at an impasse, each of us relying on what our Doctors had told us. The only way either one of us could move forward, it seemed, was to part ways. This was an incredibly painful break-up because it truly made so little sense to me, but I could not honour him without standing up for myself first.

I didn't read that sheaf of poems until I was alone and my children were both asleep. I have to admit they were not what I was expecting. I didn't grasp their full meaning at the time. They confused me. Some spoke about a man I didn't recognize through my interactions with Robert. They revealed a deep-seated depression in someone who heard voices. I hadn't read any of his work that admitted to this phenomena beforehand. I'd not seen any indication of his hearing voices or feeling, as he says in other poems, that there were tigers under the bed, or even that he had nightmares and hallucinations.

In the years since Robert Billings and I parted ways, the medical profession has grown up a lot. I mean that just the way that it sounds. No one is being told they've caught Thrush from a sexual partner these days. No one is put through that sort of trauma in their trust relationships because Thrush isn't considered to be a sexually transmitted disease any more. Rather, it's seen as opportunistic, attacking people who are physically run-down and exhausted or highly stressed. Looking it up on the internet in 2018, I discovered this explanation, at this web address:

http://www.medicinenet.com/thrush/article.htm

Thrush (oropharyngeal candidiasis) is a medical condition in which a yeast-shaped fungus called Candida albicans overgrows in the mouth and throat. Thrush may be triggered to occur by a variety of factors, including illness, pregnancy, medications, smoking, or dentures.

I was frankly hurt by the way Robert and I ended. It deeply affected my approach to relationships after that. I'd taken pride in not disrespecting my partners in the way he'd accused me of doing. Several months later, at an AGM for the LCP, I found it difficult to see him in the same room. He'd already moved on and was dating another woman, while I remained in limbo. More time passed and eventually I moved on as well. My second volume of poetry had been receiving some positive book reviews. I was not in a serious relation-ship with anyone else, but at least I'd let go of the pain.

Then I did a reading at a pub close to *Ryerson University* called *The Library* in late October 1986. Robert was in the audience. By this time, he had parted with the woman he was seeing after me. I remember he sat on the floor with his back against a wall because there was little available seating, the pub was that full. This time, I talked to him after my reading, and I was reminded of how well we used to get along. In fact, that evening, he came home with me.

The next part of this memoir is so painful I haven't talked about it before. I'm a confessional poet who has shared the details of a truly dysfunctional family. But with Robert, I felt wrongly accused of having much looser sexual morals than I possessed. Later on, after Robert had already gone, I would also feel utterly betrayed by the medical community when I discovered the true cause of Thrush.

Still, our revival on that night in October 1986 started out beautifully. Robert and I made a clear loving connection that evening. Once again, we discovered how comfortable we were with each other. In fact, the next morning, we walked to the subway arm-in-arm, me on an errand that took me to the streetcars while Robert intended to take a subway train back home. I would even say that we were both happy and delighted to have reconnected.

However, just as we got to the station, just before we were bound to part, Robert decided to ask me a question. He wanted to know if we could rekindle our prior relationship, except that he spelled it right out — referring to us as boyfriend and girlfriend — though we'd never talked about each other in those terms before.

I was both surprised and pleased, but also a bit apprehensive. Perhaps I could trust our re-connection — but I'd just come to a place in my life where I had promised to be kinder to myself, taking things slowly in my future relationships. I wanted some time to make a decision.

I said something like: "I like you a whole lot, Robert. But after the way we parted, I don't want to rush in. I need a few days to think about us."

It was clear he didn't appreciate this response. We were standing by the stairs to the train. After a brief moment, he simply turned and went down them, not even saying goodbye. His face, before he turned, had not been the only indicator for his mood. He carried dejection in the posture of his entire body. His mood shift was so dramatic, I called him back. He came up the stairs looking like a beaten dog.

I tried to explain that I wasn't saying no, that I only needed some time to think. I told him everything leading up to our parting had been wonderful, but the end of our relationship had been extremely painful for me.[1]

Robert regarded me in silence a moment before saying, "Yeah, everything looks better in hindsight." Then he turned and descended the stairs once more, refusing to turn around when I called out to him again. That was the last time I ever saw him.

Two days later, someone phoned to tell me Robert's ex-wife had just received a letter from him, saying, *'I'm going out where I came in.'* It was a day before Halloween. I knew this was being interpreted as a suicide note, that he'd been born in Niagara Falls and it was assumed he'd throw himself over the Falls. Yet, what leapt to my mind were the words he'd expressed to me about a year earlier, about the effect that a change in his habits might have — the idea that he would simply disappear if he changed what he did every day.

Immediately, I went to look for him in his neighborhood, having moved to the Bain Housing Co-op myself by then. I traced his footsteps on his last days, even as I put out a call to members of the LCP asking for donations. I wanted to hire a private detective to help search for him. I visited the owners of businesses Robert frequented, talked to waitresses and other people who saw him daily, and the money from donations gathered to just shy of $500. I even visited the places where Robert had a habit of asking for lap dances several times a week.

I need to point out that it was a different social era in the 1980s. Despite early feminism, visiting strip joints was still considered more or less acceptable for men. For many, it was even considered an ordinary, daily behavior. Robert

---

1 It needs clarifying that this conversation took place before medicine had changed its stand on Thrush. There was no new medical information yet, nothing that would allow either of us to recognize that our partner had not betrayed our bond.

wrote about strip clubs in that sheaf of poems he'd given to me, which had shocked me when I first read them. Now, in my desperation to find him, I visited several of the places he frequented, talking to the barkeep and the girls, all to no avail. No one had seen him in weeks.

Someone in the LCP gave me a reference to a private detective.

"If I locate him, what do you want me to do?" he asked. "I can't force this man to come back with me."

"I know," I said. "Just tell him that all sorts of people have donated to the fund to hire you. Tell him that we love and support him, that if he changes his mind he can come back and no one will think any less of him. That's all. He just needs to know that he's loved."

The detective quickly discovered Robert had traveled to The Briars, a favourite location where he honeymooned with Anne. Then he traced Robert to a First Nations reserve he'd stayed on for about two weeks. Yet the detective was always several days behind Robert in his movements. That was still the case when the money ran out. It was now about a month since Robert had sent that disturbing note to his ex-wife. Robert was still, apparently, alive. So I decided to relax, believing he'd decided to test his theory about what would happen if he changed his habits. Perhaps he'd found solace. Perhaps he was able to start over in a new life and make new friends.

In the meanwhile, I had applied to the Leighton Artist Colony at The Banff School of Fine Arts. I'd received a full scholarship, so I didn't have to pay for tuition, food or lodging in the Spring of 1987. Robert had been gone about six months by then. It was just a few days before I left for Banff that the media announced Robert's body had been discovered in the river below the Falls. I was devastated. I sat down to cry and I kept crying until I felt entirely drained.

I did manage to keep my commitment to six weeks at the artist colony in Banff, however, when I got there I was in for another surprise. My studio was designed by an architect who placed a cabin cruiser on stilts, half way up the side of a mountain where it would never float again. This was too ironic. On that stay in Banff, I worked in my bedroom as I simply couldn't write in that boat — not that close to the news that Robert had drowned himself.

I need to say something more about the sheaf of ten poems Robert had given to me. They are his testimony, proof of his thinking at the time. When I first read them, my own pain caused me not to see so many of the things he reveals in those poems. He keeps talking about white and light, which for Robert represents something positive. He suggests the voices he hears are falling silent, that he is learning how to speak the word love. It is not that other images, including blackness, are not there, rather that he talks so openly about that blackness. On his journey of self-discovery, Robert always delights in the moments of brightness he has dis-covered, even as he recognizes dark clouds still hover.

That sheaf of poems calls on me to say something else. I've lost many good friends and acquaintances who were authors over the years. There is one tragedy which remains constant. Whatever papers they have when their life is over — their book manuscripts and all of the pieces of their work that have not been published usually remain in boxes. In most cases, their family just doesn't know what to do with them. Meanwhile, their writing friends are too busy pursuing their own tasks to assist, or they are never asked by the family to help. This is vastly different to what occurs when a painter passes. No book publishers clamour at the studio door, anxious to buy a poet's last pages in the way that galleries will pick up a painter's last works. Their writing is packed up and put away in some family member's attic, or even a basement. Or they are simply tossed into the trash, as happened in Robert's case.

In Robert's own journey as an author, Bruce Meyer recently relayed some information I was previously unaware of. Bruce had met Robert for lunch a few short weeks before he disappeared, and Robert told him about a series of poems that he was working on "for PEN Canada and Amnesty International about torture." Though I knew nothing about it until gathering information for this book, made in his memory, I'm not surprised to hear about a second unpublished manuscript. He was a prolific author. What is truly tragic is that all of his unpublished papers were thrown out.

That brings me back to the 'new' poems in this book. I was never going to toss the ten poems I'd been given, but I certainly had no idea what to do with them for the longest time. They sat folded between the volumes on my bookshelf for many years. Then they were packed in a file folder. Finally, they were misplaced after a household move. It wasn't until I was contacted by an old school friend of Robert — Michael Clarkson — that I began to brew the idea of publishing them. By this point, I'd been operating an online literary magazine and chapbook micro-press called Big Pond Rumours for at least a decade. My first thought was to create a chapbook for Robert. But twelve poems simply were not enough for that.

When he contacted me, Michael Clarkson revealed he'd written several books on mental health. He also shared that he and Robert often talked about their depression in high school. Michael finally wrote a book centered on Niagara Falls and the great draw it has for people suffering from severe depression. He begins that book with the story of his school friend, Robert. As it turns out Michael is also a 'river man'. He's helped to fish hundreds of bodies out of the Niagara River below the surging waters of the Falls and he did go searching for his school friend.

Michael had contacted me because he was searching for people who could share insights into Robert's final motivation. He has created a film about his book and wanted to interview me for my memories of Robert. I remember telling Michael that I didn't think Robert truly understood the strength of his own work, or its power to affect people. He had little faith in his own success. Michael inspired me to honour Robert's memory by publishing those ten poems in some way, so I put out a call on Facebook.

I thought there was a chance that someone else might have a poem or two written by Robert. Or perhaps people would be willing to share pieces they wrote when we lost him. It was Richard Olafson of *Ekstasis Editions* in B.C. who said I should make the publication a *Selected Poems* with the addition of the ten 'new' poems I possessed. As soon as he said this, I knew it was the most appropriate way to honour Robert's memory.

I collected Robert's published books, and gained permission to reprint from those various publishers. I even contacted his ex-wife and gained permission to do "whatever I wanted with them", the 'them' being those uncollected poems. In this volume, each of Robert's books is presented as if it were a separate chapter in Robert's life, followed by the remaining examples from his once much larger *White City Poems* manuscript. I have even kept the order that the poems selected appeared in each of his books.

In reading all of those volumes at once, in order from the first to the last, several standard phrases presented themselves. There are images Robert uses again and again. He talks of water and stone, of black and white, or birds and winds. He speaks of daylight and darkness, love and abandonment, rivers and earth. He speaks of fish and birds in the variety of their species. He speaks of trees and flowers, also in great variety. Robert uses a third person voice much of the time, even when referring to those things he has personally discovered.

It would be a mistake to interpret the visual metaphors he uses as anything other than code for pieces of his personal worldview. They should not be read as literal representations but rather as part of his overall construction, part of his method in communicating what is in his heart. This is a man who experienced the seasons like moods and aspects of weather like modes of being. Robert offers a rare inside-view on his personal life journey, which is filled with a search for human connection around terrifying obstacles to love. He looks at himself in two forms, both positive and negative, and admits to hiding the worst of himself in his nightmares. He is at one with the landscape during the daylight hours and fearful of the impact that his personal nightmares will have upon his son. What is surprising to me is the control he had over his own behavior, so his friends didn't witness his terror, rarely experiencing more than an expression of sadness.

Bruce Meyers told me something else. Robert was working with Greg Gatenby on:

> "the IFOA when it was the Toronto International Literary Festival in 1986. There is a film, *Written on Water*, a documentary about the festival… The authors were taken to Niagara Falls for the afternoon (something Gatenby hated so he assigned the leadership of the trip to Robert). There is a shot of Robert staring at the Falls."

Bruce went on to tell me that Robert disappeared about two weeks later, suggesting a highly troubling juxtaposition of events. I am not sure Robert was contemplating his departure at that time. He was too relaxed, enjoying himself too much during his last evening with me to allow me to think he was planning his exit.

So, Robert, if you are witness to the creation of this book where you sit on the other side of this dimension, it is meant to deliver the same message I gave that private detective in 1986. Some 34 years on, it's not just myself but all of your old colleagues and friends in the LCP who want you to know: you are remembered well, for both your art and who you were as a person. You are loved. We all remember you fondly, from the time before your heart went down.

Rest in peace, Robert.

Sharon Berg
July 2020

(Above) Robert is the tallest boy in his class, standing in the back row.
(Below) From his school yearbook. Provided by Michael Clarkson.

Billings, Bob
Ambition: Newspaperwork
Probable Destiny:Writer
  of limericks for use on
  school desks
Pet Phrase: Ah, c'mon
  you guys!
Pet Peeve: Complicated
  people
Activities: Song writer,
local journalist, listen-
ing to the "Stones"

Acknowledgements:

The following pieces from his White City Poems collection were previously published in Malahat Review #79, some in slightly different form from those given to me in 1985: 1/ Colours Walking, 3/ Learning to Think, 6/ Construction, 8/ Breathing, 11/ Rain begins in the night, 12/ Smoke/Fire

My thanks go out to James Deahl, Norma West Linder, and Lynn Tait for reading a first draft of this manuscript for me. They caught a lot of the typos and gave me feedback on Robert's poetry which only served to strengthen my determination to complete this project and reintroduce his works to the world.

I also want to offer Michael Clarkson a thank you for providing several images from Robert's school days, and for letting me use a cropped section of a drawing executed by SaraLou Stuart. (The original features Michael and Robert together by Niagara Falls.)

Finally, I offer a huge thank you to Cathy Ford for the piece she wrote, which began as a back cover blurb, but as she says, *there was simply too much to say about why we still miss this man*. That much is true, whether Robert was a friend or a lover.

I am very grateful that Cyberwit decided to take a leap of faith with me and publish a book of selected poems by Robert Priest. I offer a huge thank you to Karunesh.

Permissions Note:

Details about Books by Robert Billings

blue negatives (1977) Fiddlehead Poetry Books (The press was started at the University of New Brunswick by Fred Cogswell and is now absorbed by Goose Lane Editions. 500 Beaverbrook Court, Suite 330, Fredericton, NB, Canada, E3B 5X4.

The Elizabeth Trinities (1980) Penumbra Press, Moonbeam, Ontario, Canada. Editorial: PO Box 20011, Newcastle, Ontario, Canada, L1B 1M3

A Heart Of Names (1983) Mosaic Press, 1252 Speers Road Units 1 & 2, Oakville, Ontario L6L 5N9

Trying To Dream For My Son (1984) Aureole Point Press, Toronto, Ontario, Canada. (This press was the operation of Bruce Meyer with James Deahl and Gilda Mekler. The press has now ceased to operate.)

Northern Poems: Where The Heart Catches Its Breath (1986) Penumbra Press/ Northward Journal. This could best be described as an over-sized pamphlet, rather than a chapbook of poems. (address above)

The Revels (1986) Porcupine's Quill, Erin, Ontario, Canada. 68 Main St., Box 160, Erin, Ontario, Canada, N0B 1T0

The White City Poems (1985-86) Robert was working on this manuscript when he died by suicide at Niagara Falls.

Any other poems that he wrote but did not publish 'were tossed out years ago', as happens with the last works of too many authors.

Sharon Berg

writes poetry, short fiction, novels, and academic history of First Nations education in Canada. Her poetry has been published in three full books from Borealis Press (*To a Young Horse*, 1979), Coach House Press (*The Body Labyrinth*,1984) and most recently by Cyberwit (*Stars in the Junkyard*, July 2020). She also has three chapbooks with Big Pond Rumours (2006, 2016, 2017). Her poems have appeared in Journals across Canada, in the USA, Mexico, the UK, the Netherlands, India, and Australia.

Sharon's short fiction has been published in various journals in the USA and Canada. Plus, she released her debut collection of short fiction from Porcupine's Quill (*Naming the Shadows/Stories*) in October 2019. She has also just finished her debut novel, which has the working title, *The Girl from Hungry Hollow.*

Sharon founded and edited the international literary E-Zine *Big Pond Rumours* in January 2006. It offered two issues a year of 80-90 pages each. Its pages featured poetry, short fiction, essays and book reviews until Summer 2019. She also ran a Chapbook Contest through the E-Zine, publishing Nelson Ball, Philip Elliott, Harold Feddersen, Tom Gannon Hamilton, Debbie Okun Hill, Norma Kerby, John Oughton, Wendy Maclean, Brian Purdy, and Bob Wakulich. *Big Pond Rumours Press* has also published two full books. Sharon edited, with Julie McNeill, an anthology of Phoenix Poetry Workshop members between 1976-1986 called *Paper Reunion* (2016). It was a 'paper' reunion because several members had already passed over. She also wrote a cross-genre history of Wandering Spirit Survival School called *The Name Unspoken* (2019). *The Name Unspoken* won a 2020 IPPY Award for Regional Nonfiction.